JOURNEY INTO THE DARK AND THE LIGHT

ANNABEL HARZ

JOURNEY INTO THE DARK AND THE LIGHT

Balboa Press books may be ordered through booksellers or by contacting:

Balboa Press
A Division of Hay House
1663 Liberty Drive
Bloomington, IN 47403
www.balboapress.com
1 (877) 407-4847

ISBN: 978-1-5043-0633-1 (sc)
ISBN: 978-1-5043-0634-8 (e)

Print information available on the last page.

Balboa Press rev. date: 03/16/2017

BALBOA.
PRESS
A DIVISION OF HAY HOUSE

For those in my inner circle
who witnessed the crying of my soul
and loved me anyway

CONTENTS

Light 45

PREFACE

As a teenager, I suffered from depression. As a coping mechanism, I drew pictures and wrote my feelings down. My art and poetry distilled my sadness, ultimately becoming my tools for healing as I actively used them to draw out my depression.

Reactive depression is instigated by one or more traumatic events, my counsellor, Betty, explained. In early adolescence I found myself in some adult situations involving inappropriate sexual touching. Still viewing the world from a child's perspective, I was unable to cope with these experiences. I subconsciously blocked them out until a university lecture in my teaching course detailed what sexual abuse comprises. Suddenly, images buried beneath layers of psychological protection filled my mind, and I understood in an instant what had caused me to feel apart from others—different and strange—in those formative years.

Knowing my past was the first step. The next ordeal was to conquer the depression, which had by then manifested itself as my lifestyle. This challenging process was undeniably confronting, requiring immense fortitude and inner strength I had not intuited until then—one that only a dedicated eighteen months of intensive counselling could alleviate.

Through *Journey into the Dark and the Light*, I share my experiences with the hope that others in the same situation may find themselves less desperate and less lonely than I did, garnering the comfort I lacked during my dark years. I hope that it becomes a source of inspiration for sufferers to deal with their mental illnesses in creative ways, transforming negative circumstances into those of eventual beauty by reframing them as places of learning: a passage into light and a full life.

Annabel Harz

DARK

THE FISH HOOK

What can I do
when your fish hook
catches me
and draws me to your
suffocating clutches?

Your hands are so
cold with desire,
calculated lust;
I get so scared, but I
cannot stop you.

The rape.
The helplessness.
The fish hook.

The sadness.

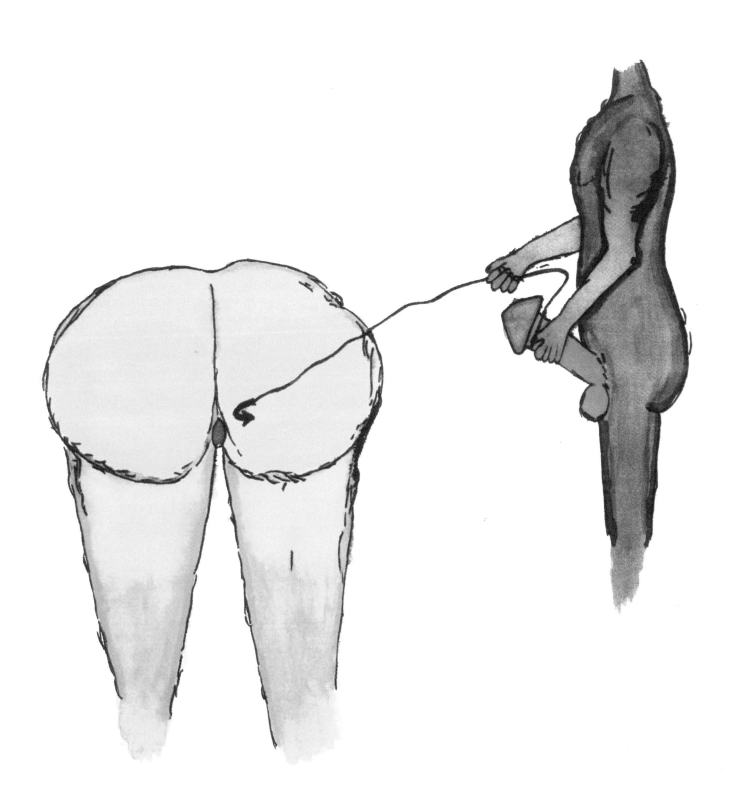

3

LOSS OF INNOCENCE

Loss of innocence
betrays childhood,
awakening the disgust of
disillusionment.

Don't you remember
when your world
was a nice place?

Why did I need to be
enlightened
so rudely,
so viciously?

It has brought me no joy.

FANTASISING MURDER

If you were a voodoo doll, a pin,
well placed, could mean the end of you.
Disappointingly, your flesh and blood
show you are human, too.

The anger I feel towards you
envelops me in rage that's blind.
My ever-increasing fury
threatens to implode my fragile mind.

I fantasise a killing—
you can play the dead,
for that is how I feel now
inside my manic head.

Will you look at me with loathsome lust,
as you have done before?
Or will your look be one of fear,
as you cower on the floor?

My demented thinking may be
irrational or purely insane.
At the least, unoriginal;
I need to free my brain.

I need to control my mind again,
take charge. Reverse the roles you won't.
I know what counts, and you, you matter
so much that you actually don't.

Our painful entanglement must alter,
lessen the suffering I endure.
I may then, finally, be free.
(Although I know I can never be sure.)

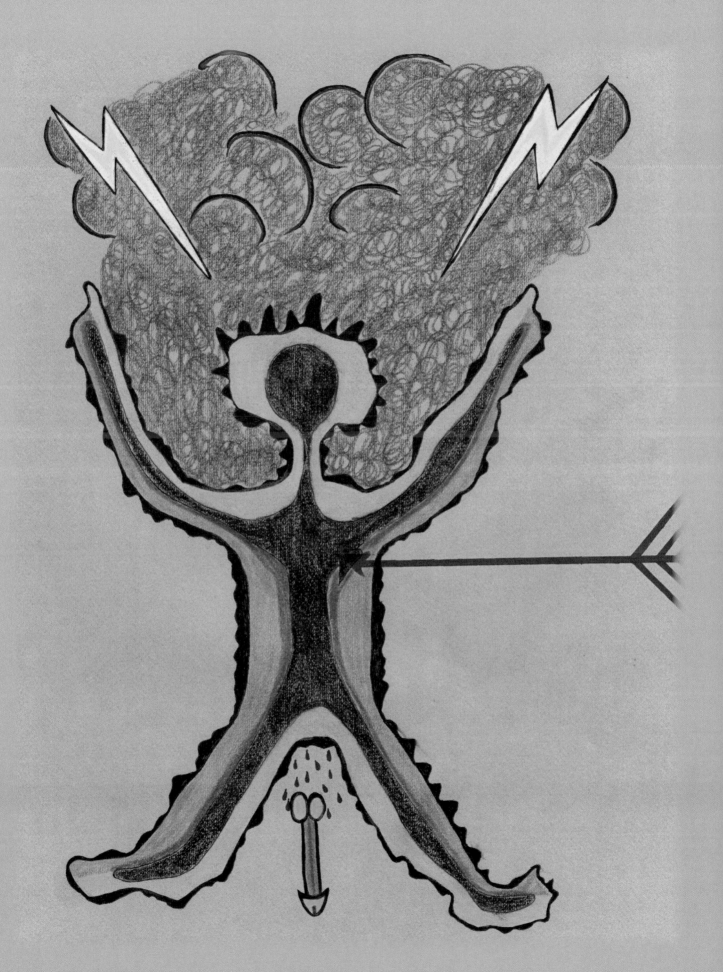

THE NIGHTMARE

I had a dream
that I woke up
and found myself living
a real life.

I'm glad it was only a dream.

MY PRESENT CONFUSION

If I were in a prism and you called out to me,
on which side would you be standing?

Would I see you or your reflection?

And if I went and then came back again,
would it be you who welcomes me
or merely a pale imitation—
one that you readily show to everyone?

I am going away.
I will return.

I hope I will be greeted with
the inside you,
the part which united with
the inside me.

And if I hear your voice
in the middle of the catacomb—
the prism that is my mind—
I will not walk towards it
immediately,
for it could just be
the echo.

No. I will wait
till I have deciphered
good from bad,
reality from pretence.

I will live, experience, find myself.
Then
I will return.

CRYING HEART/PURIFYING TEARS

Can you stop my heart from bleeding?
It is anguished,
creating an uncontrollable torrent,
a river,
a sea
of pain.

Red.
Blood.

Can you stop my heart from bleeding?
For I know not how to.

The river of tears flows on,
silent sometimes,
roaring at other times,
always flowing,
never resting.

Did I really think
if I built a boat
I could keep myself
from drifting?

I've built the boat,
in fact, I've built a few …

but I'm still
no closer to shore
than when my life was new.

Buildings and Flowers

The buildings crush the flowers,
and the flowers distort the pain;
only through the resulting tears
can I smile again.

CAGES

Tell me I am yours;
that is what I want to hear.
Tell me you'll be mine forever;
that is what I need to know.

Tell me the light of love will
never die in your eyes;
say that your passion for me is
an eternal fire,
forever burning,
replenishing the
love that grows cold
in my breast.

Tell me all this,
and I will live free—
free in the prison
that is my head.

I cry.

INVISIBLE TO YOU

I didn't know whether to
laugh or cry.
I took the safer way.

Water off a duck's back.

Flung into Memories

Dreams of strange cities and excitement.

A change in the weather flings me
into memories of times past—

Mother, happiness—

a time vague.
A time lost.

ALCHEMY

Feeling Small and Lost

My inner child cries,
"Help!"
as my outer adult
stands and watches,
unable to move,
unable to talk,
unable to assist ...

even unable to scream.

How will I find my way
out of this dark labyrinth—
what others call my mind—
if I cannot
move forward
and help myself?

The road is long, and I am weary;
I am cold, and I feel old.

What will be my salvation?
Where will I find my asylum?

Surely not inside myself,
for I feel I have meagre strength
for such a
hard journey
into the depths of my soul.

Yet, from within it must be.

Attempted Assassination of My Soul I:
THE DEATH OF MY CHILDHOOD

I fear movement, for movement acknowledges existence, and I do not wish to be right now.
For then you would see me, hear me, notice me, and you may be angry—
I also fear your wrath, your anger.

So I sit, huddled, broken, desperately hoping you won't approach me here in the corner.
I am naked.
You are immense, and I am minute—and I have absolute fear of you.

I learnt that you did not like me or want me as I was,
so I tried to change; I tried to conform,
but I could not become what you demanded.

So I denied myself and hid.

And now I relive the pain as I open the door to my past,
experiencing once again the birth of my childhood—
only to find that it died, leaving me a walking shell,
a waking memory built of pain I need never have owned. I feel so lost in the world.

It hurts to look beyond my eyes to the outside world.

I must stay small and close and tight. I must protect myself,
for my fear is great—my fear of this strange, dark place.
What is it on the brink of my memory that lets me sense the feelings but not see the events?
Who is it that opened that door? What is it that they did to me?
How did I lose my childhood? When did my childhood die?

I am deathly afraid of the answer, but I think I am ready to know; I believe I am willing to learn.
I know it's scary, but I've already survived it once.

I am ready to learn about the secrets behind the death of my beloved childhood
and the beginning of the attempted assassination of my soul.

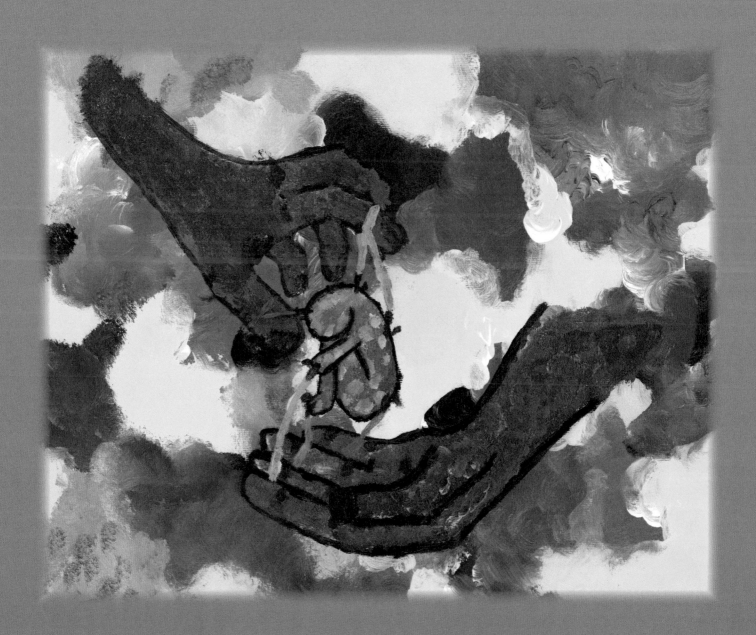

Attempted Assassination of My Soul II:
THE INSERTION OF THE KNIFE

I have a knife in my back.
It goes straight through my body
and causes my heart to bleed.

My protectors put it there
inadvertently, unknowingly,
and ever thereafter,
when something displeased them,
twisted it to make
a deeper, darker wound.

It has been hard to carry this knife in my back for so long.

I tried to remove it from my skin,
to let my life force escape.

It didn't work, and I remained.

The wound is deep and ragged now,
a very savage cut;
too many years of being wrong—
in their eyes only.

But theirs were the only eyes that mattered
because I depended on them.

It is time to take the knife out now and let the wound heal.

But can I?
Just how deep is this wound?

It feels too big to ever heal!

THE FRIGHTENED CHILD'S CREATION

I feel like a little kid
left at the side of a busy road,

and my parents went ahead
and are waiting for me to cross,
and they cannot see the cars.

I am frightened.
I need your love,
your support.

Will you stand by me on this one?

Or will I freeze from the inside?

31

The Frightened Child I:
AWARENESS

My world revolves around me
in as much as I am the centre of it.

But all that surrounds me
is in motion,
never static.

Friends drift in and out
of my life,
whether I ask them to or not.

Beyond my control is
the manner of things,
the way things are.

I am but a pulse beat
in the long, eternal life
of the universe.

Important, yet almost unnoticeable.

As I am, are other people
also pulse beats?
Some stronger, some weaker,
all vital nonetheless.

Who measures my pulse?

Who takes yours?

33

The Frightened Child II:
BEING

I am looking at my past,
holding in my hands
drawings I've done,
stories I've written
when I was young,
when I was different—
when I knew my identity.

I feel
incredibly sad
to look at my past
and sense the changes that have come,
which I do not understand.

In how many years
will I look back at
the art I create now
and think it
silly, cute, insignificant?
(Yet—always me.
Yes—always me.)

And how many tears will I shed
to know
I have changed,
yet I understand not
how or into what?

The Frightened Child III:
INITIATION OF HEALING

I know it is my journey and that nobody else can make this journey for me,
but I feel so horribly alone, cold, and unwanted.
Unneeded. Superfluous.

Rationally, I know this is not so.
But who is there when I need them most in the textured dark of a screaming night,
when my ghoulish nightmares are realised?
Can others protect me from the dangers inside my head that only
I and insanity have in common?

After all, who can protect me from myself and my depression,
which feels liberated every day, to express itself in some way?

When I go to bed at night,
I fear the wakefulness that treads on the heels of sleep, chasing it away.
Wakefulness then surrounds me, chilling me with its cold reality,
freezing the love out of my heart, and squeezing the tears out of my eyes.

Sometimes, I almost feel I could make it alone;
if I fought hard enough, my nightmares would diminish,
and the ghouls would go back to whatever hell they're from.

But that is just a blanketing cloud over the harsh sun of reality,
and that wicked sun never fails to rise.

The tiredness I feel is not from lack of sleep
but from lack of mental and emotional energy for my healing.
It is as blatant as the havoc caused,
the demons let loose,
the violent wreckage left behind
in the most private of private things I own:
my soul.

The Frightened Child IV:
FINDING STRENGTH WITHIN

Lover,
I know with unfathomable certainty that
you love me,

but at times like this
my love for myself
completes me
and
nurtures me,
and
you cannot fit in here,
as no one extraneous can;
you do not belong here,
as no one peripheral does.

I am glad that
right now
you are elsewhere,
along with
the rest of the world.

39

The Frightened Child V:
RELAPSE

If you come around to my place, I may not answer the door—
it's not that I don't love you; it's just that I'm not sure.
I see myself, and I see you, and I feel ripped apart.
But don't assume that I don't care, for that would break my heart.

You ring the bell, you tap on the window. I shut my ears to your cries.
I won't take what I can't return, unable to face my lies.
I can't bear the doors I shut in your face as I follow you with a lack of grace.
Your loving arms wish to nurture my soul, but do you understand that you can't be my goal?

I long to take you, hold you, hug you. I long to treat you with ease
but the omnipresent screaming inside my head—it does not cease.
Then I long to hide away from you, from everyone, for down inside,
I feel I'm dying. My languishing soul I heard, when every night it cried.

It cried with heartache and with pain, its stifled cry to live;
I cannot give you much, I fear, for I have so little to give.
It hurts so much to see you there with open arms, extended,
while I'm shying away from your love, which is only for me intended.

And every day, it seems like now, I'm sinking down slowly,
all alone and petrified, to the land of the dark and lonely.
I wish I could take you on this soul journey, while you'd say my eyes still shine,
but the road of triumph over despair is only ever mine.

MY SUN AND MY RAIN

for Betty

You were my sun and my rain.

I dared to show you
my frightened child,
my black and crusted little girl,
so trapped that she was dormant—

not dead,
for I still felt her pain,
but not living,
for it was only her pain that I understood.

You dared to show us that she could be
glorified in her being.
You tapped away at the shell that encased her;
you showed me how to tap and
encouraged me to try it for myself.

I found more inner resources than I ever thought possible.

With your support, I felt her come alive—
I relived our deepest pain and felt again our deepest joy.

We were reunited, and we have grown together.
Fusion.

It's been a hard journey, and I have gained
far more than I can express in mere words.

You were there to weather my storms,
to calm my fears,
to celebrate my successes
with us, my inner child and me.

You were my sun and my rain.

LIGHT

Phases of the Moon

I've always loved
the cycle of things;
I've always known
I've had the strength I needed;

I've always known,
deep within,
I could win.

I. New Moon

I am young,
but a child, emerging
from the safety of the protected womb
into the realm of the uncertain world.

I have certain security,
yet I am vulnerable,
at the mercy of the weather,
the storms of my soul.

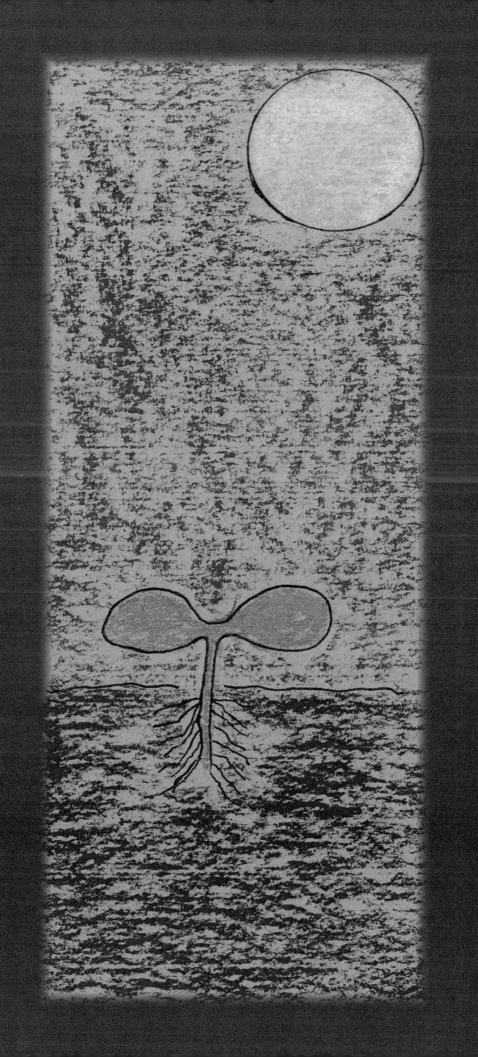

II. CRESCENT MOON

I am growing,
finding strength,
defining who I am and
who I want to be.

I remain vulnerable,
but not as much.

I gain strength
with maturity.

My roots grow stronger.

III. Oval Moon

I am beginning to be myself,
like a tree
too old to be knocked down by inclement weather,
too strong to be beaten into submission.

Myself as a tree,
an adult,
grown tall,
mature:

My new form.

IV. Full Moon

Proudly I stand:
see what I have become.

I am full-grown,
and now my changes
permeate to my surface;
they are not merely internal.

I am who I am,
and others can't decide
differently.

Now my leaves grow tenderly,
and my flowers seed
as I have come

full circle.

I'm full circle,
and I'm winning
as I spin
for the next round!

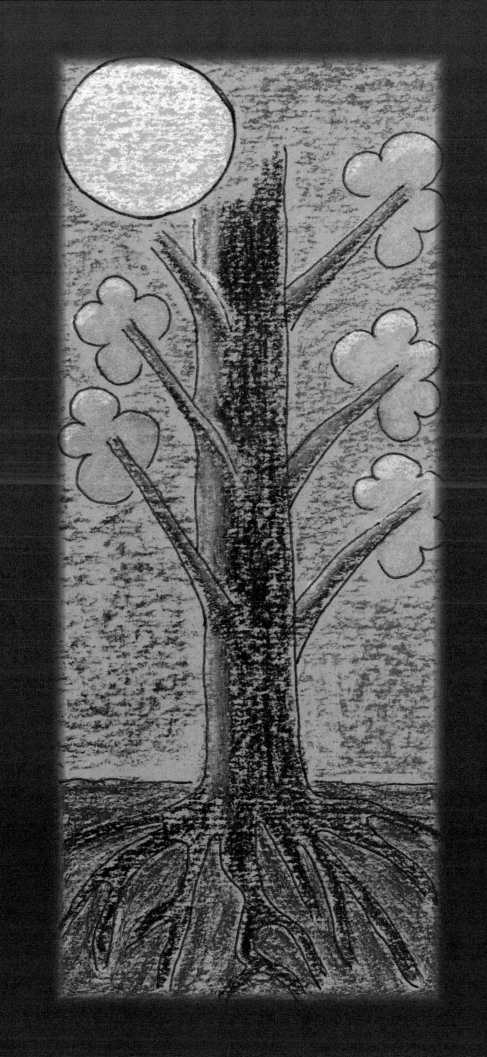

LANDSCAPES OF MY MIND

I picture the landscapes of my mind.
I travel them as I travel my moods.
Do I choose my landscapes,
or do they choose me?

I wonder—perhaps I know.

Landscape I:
SEA OF TRANQUILLITY

The land which affords,
indeed generates,
relaxation.

Landscape II:
GLACIAL MOUNTAINS OF SOMBRENESS

The creative darkness,
so textured and sad,
which my travels know so well.

Landscape III:
RUNNING RIVER OF JOY

The stark reality of happiness:
a shock to enter into,
and at what cost?

Landscape IV:
DARK SIDE FAMILIAR

The flat, shapeless plains
of mere existence,
where crying is the only comfort.

Landscape V:
CAVE OF OTHER WAYS

The only neutral landscape,
where irrationality is well known, yet foe.
Balance.

THE CARNATION

May you always be as youthful as a blossoming flower.
May your beauty radiate as you bend with the wind.
May your petals never close
And your stem never break.

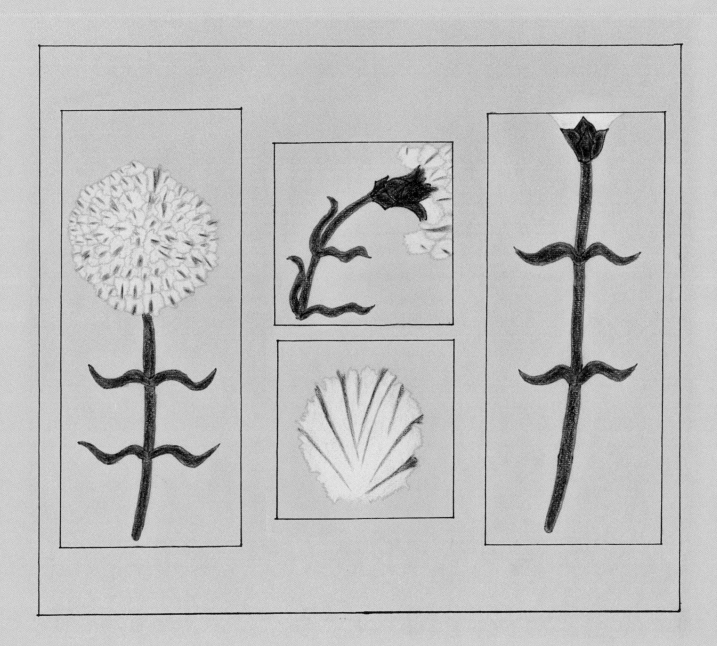

About the Author

Annabel Harz has taught primary, secondary, and adult students in public and private schools in urban, rural, and remote locations around Australia and overseas. She specialises in English, English as an Additional Language, and German.

She lives in central Victoria with her family, delighting in the country lifestyle and her creative pursuits.

Printed in the United States
By Bookmasters